I WANNA
MAKE GIFTS

by
Clea Hantman

illustrated by
Azadeh Houshyar

ALADDIN PAPERBACKS
New York   London   Toronto   Sydney

 ALADDIN PAPERBACKS

An imprint of Simon & Schuster Children's Publishing Division
1230 Avenue of the Americas, New York, NY 10020
Text copyright © 2006 by Clea Hantman
Illustrations copyright © 2006 by Simon & Schuster, Inc.

ALADDIN PAPERBACKS and colophon are trademarks
of Simon & Schuster, Inc.
Designed by Azadeh Houshyar
The text of this book was set in Providence and Bokka.
The illustrations were rendered in black pen and Photoshop.
Manufactured in the United States of America
First Aladdin Paperbacks edition October 2006
10 9 8 7 6 5 4 3 2 1
Library of Congress Cataloging-in-Publication Data
Hantman, Clea.
I wanna make gifts / by Clea Hantman ; illustrated by
Azadeh Houshyar—1st ed.
p. cm.
ISBN-13: 978-0-689-87464-2
ISBN-10: 0-689-87464-2
1. Handicraft—Juvenile literature. 2. Gifts—Juvenile literature.
I. Houshyar, Azadeh. II. Title.
TT160.H36 2006
745.5—dc22   2005019405

Clea's Dedication:
To gift-giving, love-spreading,
beauty-bestowing girls everywhere

Azadeh's Dedication:
For Azita, with love

CONTENTS

vi   the intro

CHAPTER ONE

1   classically cool gifts

CHAPTER TWO

19   surefire hits

CHAPTER THREE

39   pampering gifts

CHAPTER FOUR

57   weird & wacky gifts

CHAPTER FIVE

73   rock-'n'-roll gifts

CHAPTER SIX

83   pet-lovin' gifts

CHAPTER SEVEN

91   krazy kits

CHAPTER EIGHT

111   cool cards

CHAPTER NINE

127   bows, boxes,
    & parties aplenty

134   the outro

the intro

. . . .

I'd like to open with an ode to gift giving:

> It makes your insides all warm
> And puts a smile on your face.
> What else do you get?
> The most heartfelt embrace.

Presents are really concrete offerings of our thoughts, dreams, and well-wishing to our friends and our family. They mean that much more when we make them with our own two little hands. It sounds a little sappy, but ain't it the truth?

Gift giving should never be about going out and buying the most expensive present you can find. Or the flashiest. Or the hippest, most cutting-edge thingamabob. It should be a process that starts with thinking about the recipients, or the "givees," as I like to call them. First, concentrate on their likes and interests and personalities and hobbies. You should think about their favorite colors or their favorite music.

All these things can and should inform all your gift giving. And then, after much contemplation, you can handcraft them something that is perfect and plenty personal.

Making your gifts by hand is a fantabulous way to express your own creativity. It's an excuse to get down and dirty with the craft glue and felt and sequins. It's another chance to have fun.

Gift giving is, of course, great for holidays, but also "just because." The best gifts are often the unexpected gifts, right? No need to wait around for annual birthdays and Hallmark-deemed days of celebration. Come up with any ol' excuse to give a gift. Lincoln's Birthday? Sure! National Ice Cream Day? Why not! I Love My Friends in Canada Day? Absopositively!

And here is the extra added bonus to crafting for others: Everyone loves gifts. And everyone is grateful and will give you lots and lots of thanks and love and hugs and kisses, and hey, that's as good, or better, than the actual crafting itself. And if that's not inspiring, I'm not sure what is.

xoxo
clea

what you need
to make the projects in this book:

resourcefulness

an open heart

a great friend

a few bits and pieces

what you don't need
to make the projects in this book:

a huge wad o'cash

CHAPTER ONE

classically cool gifts

These gifts are ideal basics, perfect prezzies for most anyone on your list—thoughtful, useful, and homemade.

Project #1: coolio checkbook cover

Did you know you can buy plain ol' clear plastic checkbook covers? Do you care? Well, you should. Because in a freakishly small amount of time, you can transform one into the kind of gift that gets hugs and kisses all around. Ideal for parents, grandparents, aunts, uncles, and any other close older relatives.

What You Need

- Clear plastic checkbook cover (try stationery or office supply stores)
- Paper

The How-To

Open the checkbook cover completely and lay the whole thing flat on a table, then measure the dimensions. Cut a piece of paper to those measurements.

If you're a talented **artiste**, now is your chance to use your skills to make a boring checkbook cover shine! Draw away, covering the cut piece of paper with your art. If you can't sketch, make a collage from a few family pictures on the paper and then make a color copy of it and trim the edges. Slide it inside the checkbook cover and, um, you're done. No really, you're done. Pat yourself on the back, dearie.

• • • •

the laminator

The next Schwarzenegger blockbuster?

Not!

Doesn't it sound like it's some sort of transforming robot? And it sort of is! Basically, a laminator is a machine that seals a piece of ordinary paper in plastic, rendering it waterproof! And sturdy! And strong! And the best part? You don't need to buy a laminator, which can be way expensive. Most copy shops have them for you to use, for a small fee. Many of the projects in this book beg for you to use a laminating machine, including the next couple.

Project #2: Puckishly Perfect Place Mats

This craft—and the next one, too—utilizes one of my favorite crafty tools: the laminating machine (see page 3). It's difficult to find self-laminating sheets large enough to encase a 10-by-13-inch place mat, so you'll need to make sure your local copy shop has a laminator before proceeding.

What You Need

- A sheet of 10 x 13 piece of paper for every place mat you want to make

- Artwork to decorate the place mats (could be photos, drawings, scraps, magazine clippings, whatever)

- Glue stick

The HOW-TO

Decorate your pieces of paper. You could even decorate both sides, since they will both show. Get creative. You could glue your favorite photos to the paper. Your best drawings. Mementos from a recent family trip. Clips of the cutest guys in movies today. Whatever. Then put the decorated sheets of paper in a paper bag to protect them and take them down to your local copy shop and ask to have them laminated. The people who work at the copy shop may even let you do it yourself! You feed the piece of paper into one side of the machine, and out it slowly rolls on the other side, encased in plastic. You'll want to repeat this with the next piece of paper, and the next, until you're done.

That's it! You now have cleanable, waterproof place mats. Aren't you clever?

● ● ● ●

Project #3: Lovely Luggage Tags

Back to the laminator! Do you have a family member or friend who has to travel a lot? Then make them a homemade but extra-sturdy luggage tag. It's so simple, it won't take you much longer than it takes to get a ride to the copy shop.

What You Need

- A sheet of paper

- The recipient's address

- A few photos or a few drawings or a map

- Glue stick

- Hole punch

- A small piece of ribbon

The HOW-TO

Cut your piece of paper so it's roughly 2 1/2 x 3 1/2 inches. On one side write out the recipient's name and address in your best handwriting, or type it out on the computer and print it out on a piece of 8 1/2 x 11 paper and then trim. Maybe draw a box around it and add some doodles, if you like. Flip the paper over, and on the back side glue down a photo or a drawing or even a piece of a map. (Don't cut the map—just color copy a map and then cut **that** up!) Then take it to your copy shop and have them laminate it.*

When it's covered in plastic, trim the rectangle, leaving about a quarter inch of clear plastic all the way around. Punch a hole in one of the corners. It will take some muscle to punch through the plastic. Since you're already at the copy shop, you can always ask them if they have a heavy-duty hole punch you could borrow for a moment. Then feed your ribbon through the hole and tie it in a bow.

There you have it: the perfect little present for your favorite traveler.

*This project can also be done with self-laminating sheets, which are available at office supply stores. Simply follow the directions on the packaging.

Make It an Extra-Special Gift

Make your friend a set of tags for all their pieces of luggage!
Wrap them in tissue and put them in a little box. Or go one step
further: Wrap them up in a cheap map.

By the way, this is also a great little gift for the pal who is
moving away. Sniff.

• • • •

Project #4:
Recipe Roundup

This gift really highlights what's best about family and neighbors. I'm talking about sharing and history. This project involves a little more getting out and about and a little less crafting. But no matter, it's still a gift from the heart and totally handmade.

What You Need

- Friends, family members, and neighbors (more about this in a minute)

- Unlined 3 x 5 index cards or cardstock you've cut into even-size pieces or even a small blank journal. (Cardstock = slightly heavy paper available at art or office supply stores)

- A small piece of pretty ribbon

The How-To

Start by asking all the adults you know for their favorite, most beloved recipes. Write them down diligently. Collect as many recipes as you can. Don't forget to ask the recipe giver if there is a particular story that goes along with their dish, perhaps a personal anecdote. You could even ask for a photo of the person who originated the recipe.

Organize all the recipes into some sort of order, either by categories like "Family" and "Friends" or by style of food (for instance, "Asian Delights" and "German Favorites") or by types of meals, such as "Breakfast" and "Dinner" and "Desserts." Then begin to copy them on your cards or in your journal, using your best penmanship. If there were fun little stories that went with the recipes, add them now.

You can also decorate the cards with little doodles or even small drawings of the finished dishes. You could add any photos your family gave you. You could laminate the cards at your local copy shop or with some of those at-home, self-laminating sheets available at the office supply store. Laminating is especially great for recipe cards because it protects them from the regular spills and splatters of cooking—the cards will simply wipe clean when they're coated in a sheath of plastic.

When you've finished, stack up your cards—or close the book—and tie the whole thing up with the pretty ribbon.

Make It an Extra-Special Gift

If you've made cards, you can search out a cute old-school metal or plastic recipe box at your local thrift or antique shop. They shouldn't cost more than a couple of dollars, and they're super cute, often covered in funny retro pictures of food. If you find one that's not so cute, nab it and decorate it with pictures and beads and sparkles with a little glue.

the straight stitch

Hand stitching a small project doesn't require much in the way of equipment or skill. You just need a needle and thread and a little knowledge of a basic sewing stitch: the "straight stitch." The smaller you make this stitch, the stronger your seam will be.

Start by poking your threaded needle through the fabric from the underside and pull it through till the knot stops it dead in its tracks. Bring the needle down into the fabric again, just a quarter of an inch (or even less) away from where you first poked through. Pull firmly but not tightly—you know the diff, right? Keep doing this in even increments along your seam line. Try to keep the line of stitches very straight.

Voilá, you're sewing!

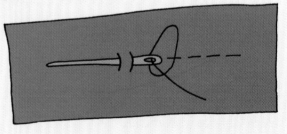

Sometimes when I know my stitches are going to show, I like to vary the stitch length. I make one long stitch, then a tiny stitch, then a long stitch, then a tiny stitch to create a pattern as I go.

When you're all done, cut the needle loose, knot your thread several times, and admire your handiwork.

Project #5: Terry cloth Beach wrap

This is a quick little gift, ideal for that friend or family member who is fond of the pool or beach. It's like a sarong, only better, because it's made from a towel. If you're looking for what I'll call a "smallish" towel, try your local mart-type store—they tend to have a few towels on the petite side.

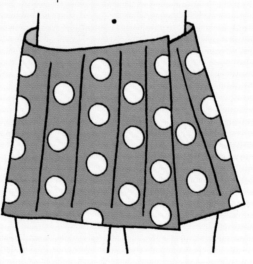

What You Need

- A smallish towel in a great color

- 3 inches of self-adhesive Velcro (available at craft stores, hardware stores, supermart-type stores in the sewing section, even some grocery stores in the paper supplies aisle)

- Needle and thread

The HOW-TO

You're going to have to guesstimate your recipient's waist measurement. Do so by wrapping the towel around another friend or family member who is about the same size as the recipient of your gift.

 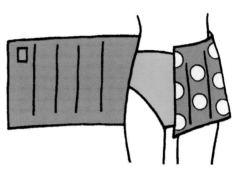

Wrap the towel around your helper's waist. Have the helper hold one edge of the towel against her body so that it is covering most of her "bikini" bottom.

Now you take the other edge of the towel and pull it taut, away from your friend's body. Stick one piece of Velcro on the inside edge of the towel part you're holding.

Now take the corner of the towel with Velcro and wrap it around the front of your friend, so that it overlaps, towel on towel.

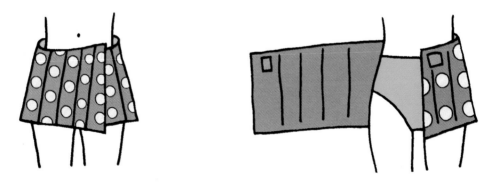

Stick the other piece of Velcro at a slight angle on the outside of the edge of towel that is flat against your friend's hip, so that it matches up and aligns with the first piece of Velcro. Fuss with the two pieces of Velcro, moving them and adjusting them until they match up nicely and fit the hips of your same-size helper.

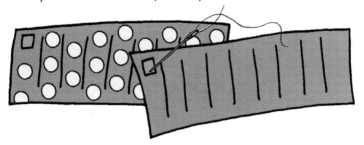

Unwrap your friend from the towel sarong and stitch the Velcro in place with your needle and thread. Velcro can be hard to sew through, so take your time. A thimble—a little metal or plastic hat for your fingers that looks like a tiny Barbie cup—will protect your thumb. But hey, there are only a few inches of sewing necessary, so don't sweat it if you can't find one. You'll be fine.

Make It an Extra-Special Gift

Make this part of a little beach or pool kit. Include a bottle of sunscreen, a great paperback novel, and a pair of funky sunglasses. Throw them all into a cheap mesh beach bag and tie a bow on top. It's not just a gift—it's an excursion!

Project #6:
Seriously Super (Sun)Glass Case

Pair this gift up with a snazzy pair of
sunglasses or give this gift alone to
someone who wears glasses or sunglasses
all the time. The neato-keeno little spin
on this here case is that we're going to
use lens-cleaning cloths on the inside,
so the recipient can always have
sparklingly clean glasses wherever
they go!

What You Need

- Two pieces of 4 x 7 inch felt

- An eyeglass cleansing cloth—at least large enough to cut
  two 4 x 7 pieces from it (you should be able to find such
  cloths in the pharmacy area of any drugstore)

- Pinking shears (those fun scissors that cut a zippy
  zigzag edge)

- Straight pins
- Needle and thread

The HOW-TO

Cut two 4 x 7 inch rectangles from the cleansing cloth. Make a felt sandwich with the two cleansing cloths inside. Pin along the edges of three sides, leaving one of the shorter sides open and unpinned. Cut along all four sides with the pinking shears, cutting through all the layers as you go and staying as close to the edge as possible.

Thread and knot your needle. Sew a basic straight stitch just on the inside of the zigzag, starting on a long side. Sew up that long side, then go across a short side, and finally, go down the other long side, leaving the final short side open—so the givee can slip their glasses inside easily.

Guess what? You're done. But feel free to decorate this gift with any number of things, like buttons or feathers or glitter and glue.

CHAPTER TWO

surefire hits

These gifts are fun, exciting even—but not too kooky. They're personal enough that they make a lovely little statement to the givee about how much you care.

Project #1:
Mighty Mini-Magnets

There are a ton of ways you can make little magnet gifts. This is my favorite.

What You Need

- Scraps of felt

- Fabric glue or embroidery needle and thread

- Small magnet disks (try the office supply store or large craft mart)

The How-To

Place two pieces of felt together—they don't have to be the same color—and then cut a small rudimentary animal shape, like a bunny head or a basic fish shape, out of both pieces at once. Then place the little magnet disk between the two cutout pieces and either glue the edges of the two pieces together or sew all the way around the edges, securing the magnet inside. I like the latter approach because you can use contrasting-colored thread and get a really crafty finish. Attach a pair of eyes and a mouth with more felt scraps, or simply sew little X's with your thread in place of the eyes. The end result is a vaguely anime-style animal that is way cute and super lovable.

Make It an Extra-Special Gift

Create a little menagerie of these adorable magnets and then present them in a metal box, so they "stick" to their container. But where to get a metal box, you ask? Try the tin box your favorite mints came in!

• • • •

another easy and adorable magnet gift

involves gluing those same little magnet disks to the backs of pretty seashells. If your seashells are fairly ordinary, you might make 'em extra sweet by painting them fantastic colors or even, if you're so inclined, painting little scenes on them. Glue the magnet disks on the backs of the shells. Place a few of these in a larger seashell, wrap the whole thing up with netting or tulle, and voilá! Beauteous gift for your favorite beach lover.

Project #2:
The Monogram Stamp

Imagine having a stamp with your name written out all fancylike. Or your monogram. Or your name **and** address. You could stamp it onto faux business cards or envelopes that beg for your return address. You could stamp it inside all your books to claim ownership. Or all over your notebooks. This is a thoughtful, curious little gift and while not entirely homemade, close enough. You could give this gift to almost anyone. Just think about how each recipient would use such a gift and tailor the design accordingly.

What You Need

- A computer and printer (but honestly, you could pull this off without one)

- Your imagination

The HOW-TO

On your computer open up a design program or even a word-processing program that has fun fonts. Think about what you would like the stamp to say. It could be faux serious and say **From the Desk of** _____ and then the person's name. Or it could be simple and feature only their initials. You could use a whole address, as in a return mailing address, or you could use just the givee's name and e-mail address so he or she can stamp it on little giveaway friendship cards. Add a simple but eye-catching design around the border or next to the name, if your program has that capability. Or draw a border with a pen after you print out the text. Print out your final pièce de résistance exactly the size you'd like the stamp to be.

You could also write out the givee's name with a good thick pen like a Sharpie, skipping the computer and printer altogether—but make sure you keep your lines clear and simple.

Look up "Rubber Stamps" in the Yellow Pages and peruse the listings for places that make custom stamps. Many old-school stationery stores do this, as will specialty rubber-stamp shops. Making a stamp will cost you in the neighborhood of $10 to $20, provided your stamp isn't huge, and it will take less than a week to produce. When you go to pick it up, test it out before paying to make sure the design came out just as you hoped it would.

Gorgeous, useful, **and** thoughtful—everything you want in a gift!

Make It an Extra-Special Gift

Pick up a handful of stamp pads (make sure they are the right size for your stamp) in your recipient's favorite colors and wrap them all together using "wrapping paper" you make by inaugurating the new stamp all over some plain paper!

• • • •

Project #3:
Brainy but Beloved Bookmarks

There are a muncha-buncha ways you can make bookmarks. They make great gifts on their own, or you can put them inside a favorite novel or craft book (like this one!). You could even put them in a notebook or sketchbook (see the fourth project in this chapter).

For a quick and easy bookmark, just find a length of supercool, supersturdy ribbon and cut it to classic bookmark size (about 1 1/2 inches by 8 inches). Finish the ends by trimming them into an inverted point with pinking shears (those fancy scissors that make zigzag edges)—you know, so they look like snake tongues. If the ribbon isn't sturdy, glue a strip of cardstock between two layers of fancy ribbon.

If you want a more involved and slightly more personal bookmark, I've got an idea for you....

What You Need

- Two scraps of felt in contrasting colors
- A very small picture you'd like to include on the bookmark (a photo or a clipping of a hottie from a magazine)
- Glue
- Double-sided tape
- Pinking shears
- Piece of cardstock
- Contrasting embroidery thread and needle (optional)

The How-To

Take your two pieces of felt and stack them one on top of the other, with the cardstock sandwiched in the middle. Cut the whole thing into a rectangle measuring 3 by 10 inches. Take the piece of felt you want to be the top and fold it vertically in half. Cut out a half-heart shape, a very, very small one, perhaps only a half inch wide or less. Open it back up to reveal a full and perfectly symmetrical "heart hole." Take your photo and place it behind the heart hole, and look—it's like a little frame!

Now, if you're gonna use the embroidery thread, read on; but if you're not, skip to the next paragraph. I just use embroidery thread as an accent. Thread the needle and knot the end of the thread. I start on the underside of the top piece of felt, sticking my needle through the back of the bottom point of the heart. Then I make basic, even straight stitches all the way around the heart. Make sure to end on the back side too, so the end knot can stay hidden inside the bookmark. Trim the knot closely. You could add a monogram—you know, an initial or a flower. Whatever you want to "stitch" onto the felt, do that now. Then proceed to the next paragraph.

With your double-sided tape, affix the picture to the cardstock so it will align with the "heart frame" when you cover it with the other piece of fabric. With another piece of sticky tape, attach the top piece of felt to the cardstock. Now your photo should peek through perfectly. Spread some glue on the back of the cardstock and glue it to the back felt piece, then do the same for the front. Place a heavy book on the bookmark to smoosh the pieces of felt together—this will help set the glue. Give it a few minutes to dry.

Now your bookmark is starting to take shape, but it still needs to be trimmed. You could mark out straight lines with a ruler and pencil on the felt, or you could just wing it. Take your pinking shears and cut all the way around the bookmark. The end product should be approximately 1 1/2 x 8 inches.

You're done.

Cute, no? Wrap it up all by itself, or give it with the gift of a book.

● ● ● ●

Project #4: The Notebook OR CD Case OR Photo Album OR Sketchbook OR Day Planner

Now, **that's** a mouthful. Let me explain. This fairly basic craft can be any number of things depending upon what kinds of pages you fill the "book" with. You could make any of these lovely items:

- A school-type notebook

- A multiple CD carrier/book

- A photo album

- A sketchbook

- A day planner

The how-to is the same for all. The outside materials are the same. It just comes down to the insides—that is, what makes each thing a "thing." It's hard to explain, but it'll become clearer as we go, I promise.

What You Need

- A local copy shop that offers spiral binding (most do)

- A cover for your notebook/CD book/photo album/sketchbook/ day planner; this could be any of the following things:

  - Cereal box or similar cardboard box (as for granola bars, cookies, that sort of thing)

  - Old record album cover

  - Old paperback book cover

  - Thick and hearty pages from an old book

  - Comic book covers

  - Plain box cardboard

  - Cardstock, plain or fancy

  - Basically, anything that is thin enough that you can punch a hole in it and thick enough to make a reasonably sturdy cover

- That's it for the cover. Now for the insides. What you will need depends on what it is you're going to make, so . . .

  - If you're going to make a NOTEBOOK, you'll need 50–100 sheets of lined paper.

  - If you're going to make a CD CASE, you'll need 15–40 pages of plastic CD sleeves (available at office supply stores).

  - If you're going to make a PHOTO ALBUM, you'll need either 20–40 sheets of black construction paper and a small bag of photo corners OR 20–40 pages of "picture sleeves," available at office supply stores and stationers.

- If you're going to make a SKETCHBOOK, you'll need 40–80 pages of either plain white paper or slightly textured drawing paper (available at art supply stores).

- If you're going to make a DAY PLANNER, you'll need a packet or two of day planner refill pages, also available at the office supply store.

The HOW-TO

If you're making a CD case or day planner, you'll need to make your book the size of the sheets you'll be inserting. If you're making a notebook, sketchbook, or photo album with black construction pages, your books can be any size you want. Just make sure the cover is cut so that it is half an inch larger than the inside sheets on the **top, bottom,** and **right side only.** Do not factor in the extra half inch on the left side—you want the left side to line up perfectly.

Once you've trimmed your cover and/or pages to the perfect size, just take it all down to your local copy shop. They will punch the holes needed and fit your new book with a spiral binding. Ask if they have metal ones—they're super cool. But if they don't, plastic will do nicely.

That's it! No really, that's it.

And the binding shouldn't cost you but a few dollars per book, tops.

Make It an Extra-Special Gift

If you made your pal a notebook, add a Bizarro Girly Pencil (page 64). If you made your friend a CD case, make her a CD and throw it in a sleeve before you wrap up the case. If you made your loved one a photo album, fill the first page or two with your favorite pictures. If you made your kid sister a sketchbook, throw in a small box of colored pencils or chalk. And if you made your compadre a day planner, include a bookmark to go along with it (see the previous project in this chapter).

• • • •

Project #5: The Keepsake Envelope Book

This is a sweet gift for that sentimental friend or family member. Basically, you gut a hardcover book (I know, I'm not a fan of destroying books—but you can remove the text intact so that it's still readable later on). Inside the empty hardcover shell you'll tape a series of envelopes—specific instructions will follow. This serves as a special sort of file for mementos and keepsakes like ticket stubs, odd-size photos, scraps, articles, poems—anything.

While this project is totally sweet, as I mentioned before, it's also **way** cool, especially if you get your hands on a hip hardcover book. Check the used bookstores. I'm partial to old Nancy Drew novels—they're the perfect size for classic "card-style" envelopes, which are usually just a quarter inch shy of 5 x 7. And yes, the instructions are extensive, but in reality, this isn't a hugely time-consuming project, and after the first couple of "pages," once you really get the hang of it, this project moves along quick as lightning!

What You Need

- A hardcover book, preferably about 5 x 7 inches and hopefully no thicker than, oh, 1 inch

- 14—20 envelopes (depending upon how thick your book is—you're going to fill the book with 'em); they can be white or colored, but they must be slightly smaller in length and width than your hardcover book

- Bookbinding tape or colored masking tape or some other colored tape that is no wider than 1 inch (you should be able to find colored tape at the local art store)

- 1 foot of coordinating ribbon

- 1/8 yard of felt in a coordinating color to go with the book cover

- Craft glue

- Those little sticky-backed disks of Velcro, no bigger than 1 inch each, preferably even smaller (optional)

The HOW-TO

Start by removing the pages from the book—the aforementioned "gutting." If you're using an older book, it's quite simple because back in the day when the bookmaking folks would bind a hardcover book, they didn't glue the pages to the binding; they glued or sewed the pages together as one piece. You start removing the text by opening the book so that the inside cover is on the left and the first page is on the right. Now run your scissor tip along the middle: the "spine" of the book. The pages should separate from the cover effortlessly.

Now flip to the back of the book so the inside back cover is on the right and the last page of the book is on the left. Do the scissor tip thingy again and poof! Like magic, your text should come out in one piece.

If your book is rather new, the process may be a little different. The pages may be glued right to the spine, in which case you'll have to take a butter knife and carefully wedge the blunt tip into the spine. Work the knife back and forth. This will break the glue's seal from the spine and allow you to pull the text from the cover.

Take the text and place it by your bed—you'll start that book tomorrow. For this project all you need is the cover. But you can set that aside just now.

If you're going to use the Velcro disks, add them now. Essentially, you would use the Velcro to "secure" the envelopes so that the envelopes would be reusable. Simply stick one piece of the Velcro disk on the underside of the envelope's pointy flap and then stick the other corresponding piece on the envelope itself. Repeat this with all your envelopes—or skip this part altogether.

Now grab those envelopes and your tape....

Lay the first envelope down so the part you address—the front side—is facedown. I'm going to call this "Envelope A." You see the flap, right? Turn the flap of Envelope A so that when opened flat, it points to the left.

Lay the second envelope (you got it, "Envelope B") with the part you'd write your friend's address on facing up, but make sure that if you were to open the flap, this one would point to the right.

Align the right edge of Envelope A with the left edge of Envelope B, but don't overlap them. Take a piece of tape cut to the length of the envelopes and place it on top of the "seam," so that half the tape is on Envelope A and half the tape is on Envelope B.

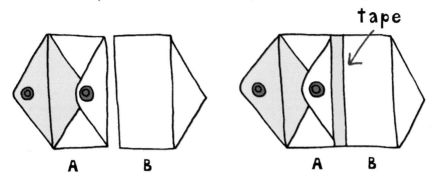

Voilá, your first two pages are "bound."

Now you're going to repeat this process, adding more "pages." Start by folding Envelope B to the left so it lays on top of Envelope A. The original Envelope B becomes the new Envelope A as you add the new "page." Lay the third envelope with the part you address faceup and again make sure that if you were to open the flap, it would point to the right. Align the edges and tape the seam.

Keep adding envelopes in this manner till you have enough to fill about three quarters of the spine. You want to leave a little room because you're inviting your givee to fill these envelopes with stuff.

Once you've assembled all your "pages," it's time to attach them to the cover. Now, remember what I said about how bookbinding people used to bind books without adhering the pages to the spine? That's exactly what we're going to do. We're going to attach just the first page to the inside front cover and just the last page to the inside back cover. And we do this in pretty much the same way we attached the envelopes to each other—using a piece of tape that covers the "seam" between the cover and the page.

Open the hardcover wide and lay the front and back covers totally flat. Take your "envelope pages" and place them on the right side

of the cover, aligning the left edge of the envelopes with the
left side of the spine. Apply a strip of tape to the seam so that
it is half on the hardcover and half on the top envelope. Flip all
the pages to the left. Align the right edge of the last envelope
with the right edge of the spine. Nab another piece of tape and
seal the seam for the last time.

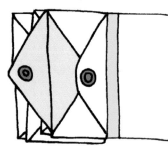 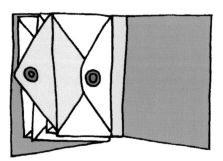

Once you've done this, give the book a good open and shut
movement, then crunch the spine if you need to get it all flexible.
The tape can handle it.

You could stop there, but the inside of the book cover may have
someone's name on it, or it may have ripped a little when you
gutted the book. Not too pretty. That's when the felt (and ribbon)
comes into play.

Cut a piece of felt the same size as the inside of the book cover.
If you have pinking shears, you could edge the felt in a lovely
zigzag pattern, but it's not necessary. Cut a second piece of felt—
this one is for the back inside cover. But before you glue the felt
down, stop.

What about the ribbon?

Well, the ribbon is going to stick out horizontally from under the
felt on the front inside and back inside covers and meet where
the book opens. You can then tie it in a bow! To do this, cut your

foot of ribbon in half. Glue about 1 inch of one end of the ribbon to the inside front cover, about halfway down. Repeat this on the back cover, making sure the two pieces of ribbon line up.

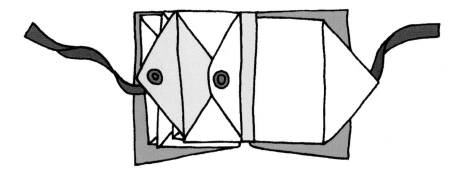

Now for the felt!

Cover the inside front cover of the book with a thin layer of glue. Line up the top edge of your felt piece with the top edge of the inside cover and smooth it down on the glue. Repeat this on the back inside cover.

You are now officially done. Let it dry, then tie that ribbon in the cute bow I mentioned before. Wow. What a gift!

Make It an Extra-Special Gift

I think this one is already pretty darn special, but if you wanna go the extra mile, you could do a couple of things. For starters, you could add a couple of mementos or pictures inside the envelopes. Or you could get out your best pen and either start drawing on the front sides of the envelopes or writing little notes for your friend in fancy calligraphy-inspired handwriting. Or poems. Or just things you love about that person.

Oh, it makes my heart zing, I tell you!

CHAPTER THREE

pampering gifts

These gifts are meant to indulge the recipient and make them feel incredibly special. Plus, everyone loves to relax, so these items are more special (and much cheaper) than a spa gift certificate!

Project #1: A Happy Little Hand Warmer

This is a perfect gift for those who live in cold country or for those friends and family who always have cold hands. (For those loved ones who have cold feet, see the slippers project in this chapter too.)

I like the idea of recycling an old thrift store cashmere sweater for this project, but you could also buy the smallest piece of high-quality wool felt the fabric store will allow—usually about a quarter yard, which is enough for three hand warmers. You don't need a sewing machine, but you do need a few basic hand-sewing tools like a needle and thread.

What You Need

- A thrift store cashmere sweater or a small amount of very fine wool felt

- Needle and thread

- Ceramic pie weights (available at kitchen stores and sometimes at big chain stores in the kitchen department; these tiny little ceramic balls can be heated up)

- Embroidery floss in an attractive color and an embroidery needle (optional)

The How-To

Okay, we're essentially making a palm-size beanbag that can be heated up in a microwave oven. This in mind, cut out two 4-by-5-inch pieces of cashmere or felt (if you're making these for someone who has small hands, decrease the size a bit; conversely, if the person has extra-large hands, go ahead and increase the size). Sew the two pieces together on three sides using a basic straight stitch. Turn the little bag right side out, so the stitches aren't showing. Fill it with about half a cup of the ceramic pie weights, tuck the edges of the last side in, and finish this last side with a hemstitch (see the sidebar on page 42).

Alternately, you could purchase a pair of new, fluffy woolen socks and cut the toe part off, about midarch. Toss the ankle/leg part. Stuff the toe part with the ceramic pie weights and then sew up the only open seam. This would reduce your sewing time a bit.

Either way, this is a useful gift that shows genuine thought and concern for the recipient.

Don't forget to include a tag with the instructions! Something like: Next time you're feeling cold, place this handmade hand warmer in the microwave. Heat the warmer on high for five minutes. Remove from the microwave and snuggle with the warmer.

Make It an Extra-Special Gift

Along with the hand warmer and instruction card, include a cute can of hot cocoa mix and a sweet mug for the perfect cold-busting present.

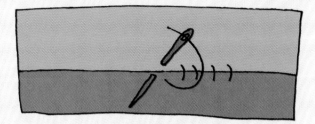

the ever-useful hemstitch

This is the way to finish off a hem on a skirt or a curtain, but it's also a great way to finish the last side of a sewing project that you began sewing when it was turned inside out, like a pillow or a small ceramic pie weight beanbag.

When you're finishing the final side of a project, you begin by folding the raggedy raw edges of both of the pieces of fabric you're stitching together inward, essentially hiding the raw edge. Press it with a hot iron.

Stick the point of the needle down in the fold, between the two pieces of fabric, and pull it through to the outside. We do this to hide the knot.

Sew the two pieces together by making teeny-tiny diagonal stitches that stretch from one fold to the other, joining them together. But you don't want to go through the fabric carelessly. Instead, you poke the needle through the fabric gingerly. The goal is to only really get a couple of threads of the fabric with each stitch. Sure, you may be able to see the stitches when you look closely, but they will be far more hidden than if you had just sewn a basic straight stitch.

Project #2: Rippin' Rice Neck Roll

Ahh, the power of the microwave. I'm really not a fan of them for cooking stuff, but for creating a little warmth when there is none, there is nothing better.

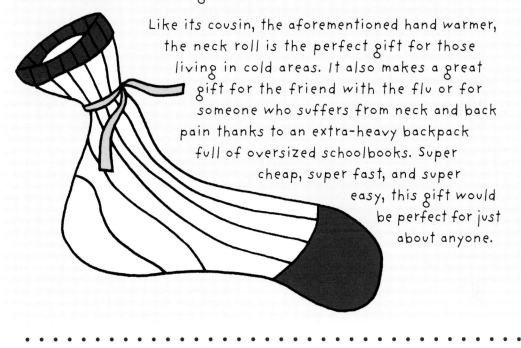

Like its cousin, the aforementioned hand warmer, the neck roll is the perfect gift for those living in cold areas. It also makes a great gift for the friend with the flu or for someone who suffers from neck and back pain thanks to an extra-heavy backpack full of oversized schoolbooks. Super cheap, super fast, and super easy, this gift would be perfect for just about anyone.

What You Need

- A new, soft, clean sock (must have a tight weave, no frilly open-weave socks here—it needs to be long enough to rest comfortably on the back side of your neck, but it doesn't need to be long enough to wrap around to the front; so, um, no Peds, but any other sock variety is probably great)

- A little piece of yarn
- A bag of uncooked rice

The How-To

Take your sock and fill it most of the way with uncooked rice. Tie a very tight knot around the opening with a length of yarn. Add a bow if you like, but make sure the knot is very tight, doubled and tripled and quadrupled. (Can you imagine the rice busting out of a weak knot? Oh, the horror! The mess!)

Guess what? You're done!

Just write out a lovely little instruction card telling the person to place the roll in a microwave, on high, for one minute. And then they can place the roll on their shoulders if their muscles ache. Or on their neck if they're sick. Or anywhere that's a little chilly. Advise the givee to keep it stored in a plastic bag (to avoid moths chomping on their present). It can be used over and over and over again, anytime they feel cold or sick or achy.

Now brace yourself for the pinched cheeks and the squishy hugs you'll get from the recipients, who can't believe you made such a considerate gift.

Make It an Extra-Special Gift

For every pair of socks you buy, make a matching heartwarming set: a hand warmer **and** a rice neck roll. Use one whole sock for the roll and the toe of the second sock for the hand warmer. Place them together in a box with the instructions for each. It's like thoughtfulness in a box.

Project #3:
Sweet-Smellin' Sachets

You probably have a relative or
friend who is all about "pretty."
You know what I mean—they
like things to smell fresh and
flowery; they like
long, silky baths;
they like everything
to be rosy. Well,
here is the gift for
them. And it's easy.
Unbelievably easy.

What You Need

- A small square of plain cotton fabric
  (a scrap would be A-OK)

- A pretty handkerchief

- A piece of ribbon
  (a scrap would be A-OK here, too)

- A small bar of deliciously scented soap

The HOW-TO

Lay the handkerchief facedown. Center the scrap of cotton fabric on top and place the bar of soap in the center. Gather all the sides of the hanky, encapsulating the soap and cotton scrap in the process, and tie it all up with the ribbon.

There it is: an instant sweet-smelling sachet just perfect for your loved one's dresser drawer. And oh-so-pretty!

Make It an Extra-Special Gift

Just make up a bunch of these sachets with hankies of different colors and soaps in various scents. Attach a little tag to each one, suggesting where it should be put, like inside a sock drawer or in a closet, near shoes. Put them all in a pretty little box, and you have a good-size gift that cost very little money and took even less effort.

• • • •

Project #4:
Stupendously Sweet Slipper Socks

Everyone needs slippers, right? Cozy slippers, the kind that feel like a great pair of socks. So why not make them **out** of socks? Hey, socks are generally cheap!

Now, if you have the same size feet as the recipient, this will be easy; you can stand in as the foot model. But if not, you're going to have to be sneaky and "borrow" an insole from one of their shoes. Just make sure you put it back!

What You Need

- A pair of incredibly cozy, warm socks

- A piece of cardboard

- A sheet of fusible web tape (the type labeled FOR APPLIQUÉ comes in a roll, which is ideal; you'll have no problem finding this at your neighborhood fabric or craft store)

- 1/4 yard of sueded fabric—I'm not talking about suede, as in leather; sueded fabric refers to any material with a fuzzed, suedelike texture (you'll find this at the fabric store, natch)

- An iron

- A sewing pencil (it's basically a pencil that shows up on fabric; if you don't have one, you can wing it with an ordinary-type pencil—your lines will just be harder to see)

The How-To

Using the cardboard, make a template of the person's foot using either your foot or the nabbed insole. Do this for both a left and a right foot (you can take just one insole and flip it over for the opposite foot's silhouette). Now take your right and left foot templates and trace around them on both the sheet of fusible web tape (on the paper—don't remove the paper just yet) and on your fabric. Cut out both the fabric and the fusible web tape along your pencil lines.

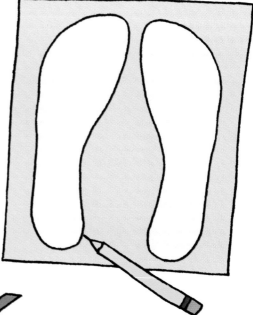

Now slide one of the original cardboard templates you made inside one of the socks. Fiddle with it till it's creating a "sole" for the sock in just the right place. The sole should be faceup now. Place the fusible web tape "footprint" down first on the bottom of the sock, then the sueded fabric "footprint" on top of that, lining it all up. Iron on a low setting (or as directed on the fusible web tape packaging) and go over the edges twice. Repeat with the other sock.

Remember to turn off and unplug the iron, then remove the cardboard from the inside of the socks. Voilá, brand-new slipper socks extraordinaire!

Make It an Extra-Special Gift

You can make these slipper socks with silly socks, too, like those toe socks that have separate little mini-socks for each tiny toe. Instead of attaching the fusible web tape and sueded material to the whole sole, you would stop just short of the toes, then you would make an extra piece just for the big toe! Hee! I'm laughing just thinking about it.

Project #5:
A Treat of a Teacup Candle

In need of a pretty, sweet-smelling, "loverly" little gift to say thanks to Mom or Grandma or even your frilliest friend? The answer is in a teacup. At just about any thrift store you'll find a few lonely, orphaned teacups. They should cost you less than a buck each. You do need two important things from a craft or candle-making store: wicking and wick sustainers. The latter are the little metal jobbies that hold the wick to the bottom of the cup. Oh, and wax gets really hot, so be careful. And don't be afraid to enlist a friend or family member to help out with this one.

What You Need

* Two saucepans—one must be able to fit inside the other

* A handful or two of half-burnt candles (or, alternately, some cheap candles)

- Wicks and wick sustainers, one of each for every teacup
- A candy or candle thermometer (you can find the latter at a candle-making supply shop or craft store)
- Kitchen tongs
- Long wooden skewers
- A couple of beautiful vintage teacups

The HOW-TO

Take the bigger of the two saucepans and fill it one third of the way with water. Warm the water over medium heat until it is simmering (in other words, boiling quietly and emitting teeny bubbles). Place the half-burnt candles in the smaller saucepan and place **that** inside the first saucepan. The simmering water will melt the candles in the smaller pan slowly and gently, so they won't burn and stick like glue to the bottom of your pan. Clip your thermometer to the side of the pan (use only a candy or candle thermometer for such a job) and try to keep the wax at about 180 degrees. If the temperature is a lot lower, kick up the heat a bit; if the temperature is flying way high, turn it down.

Once the candles have burnt down to a liquidy, waxlike consistency, carefully pull the old wicks out with those tongs. Go slow—you don't need dripping, hot wax getting on you or anything else. Now throw those wicks away.

Next, nab your pretty teacups. Measure and cut a piece of wicking deep enough to stick out the top of your teacup, plus a couple of inches just in case; we can always cut the thing shorter when we are done. Stick one end of the wick through the center hole of the metal wick sustainer and pinch. Tie the other end to the center of a wood skewer.

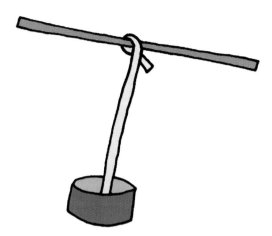

Holding the skewer horizontally, dip the metal wick sustainer in the melted wax, pull it out, and then stick it to the bottom of your first teacup. The skewer can rest across the top of the teacup, keeping your wick vertical. If the wick is sagging, just roll the skewer gently till the wick is relatively taut.

Pour the wax into the cup **very** carefully. This is where your lovely assistant might come in handy. Stop about half an inch from the top edge of the cup. Repeat this with the other cups.

Clean up your mess while the candles harden, which should take about an hour. When they're all dry, untie the skewers and trim the wicks so they peek out about an inch from the tops of the candles.

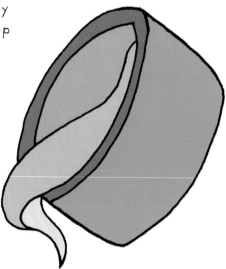

You could stop here, but your candles
will have what is called a "well"
around the wick—that's a little
sunken hole in the center. I think
it looks fine, but if you want them
to have a clean, flat top for that
professional look, here's what
you do: Poke the tip of a
skewer all around the wick,
leaving a circle of pinprick-size
holes. Then pour in some more melted
wax, just a smidgen, until the top evens out and is just a little
higher than it was before. (Yeah, you've got to melt the wax
again—so is it worth it? Up to you.)

Make It an Extra-Special Gift

You know how matches sometimes come in cute little boxes that
slide apart to reveal the sticks? Nab a couple and cover them in
pretty paper or simply paint the boxes. Include them in a package
with the teacup.

* * * *

Project #6:
Fetching Flower Forcing Can

Do you know someone who likes
flowers? These flowers will last a
bit longer than the cut variety. In
fact, they'll grow and bloom!

What You Need

- 1-quart plain, empty paint can (available at the hardware store)

- Some cute wrapping paper or clippings from a magazine you like

- Double-sided tape

- Piece of plain paper

- Pen

- A couple of scoops of sand (again, try the hardware store)

- Two or three flower bulbs like paperwhites or another variety of narcissus

- A dishcloth (not to give away, just to use for a moment)

- Hammer

The HOW-TO

Start by covering the paint can with the wrapping paper or magazine clippings (alternately, you could paint the can). Use the tape to affix each scrap to the can. Cut a circle of plain paper that will fit on the can's lid. Write a greeting or draw a picture. Attach it to the can's top with your double-sided sticky tape.

Pour the sand in the can, filling it halfway. Place your bulbs in the sand, roots down and pointy bits up. Write some instructions on a little piece of plain paper. Something like: **Want them to bloom? Take the lid off, drip-drop some water in till the sand is nice and moist. Put on a windowsill or some other sunny place. Wait about 6—7 weeks and voilá...fetching flowers!**

Roll up your instructions like a teeny-tiny scroll and place them inside your can. Put the lid on. Toss your dishcloth on top and gently hammer along the can's edges to seal it up. Now go put that dishtowel back in your mom's cupboard. (I mean, if it isn't dirty.)

• • • •

CHAPTER FOUR

weird & wacky gifts

. . . .

Sometimes we have a friend or a family member for whom a traditional gift just won't do. That's when you turn to the "Weird & Wacky" section of this book. These are ideas that will satisfy the person who has everything or the person who just likes their stuff a little...**different.**

. . . .

Project #1: collage Tarot Deck

This is a large undertaking—there are seventy-eight cards in a traditional tarot deck, after all. But if you have a pal who loves reading people's cards or who has been aching to get into such a hobby, then this is the perfect present. The end result is truly personal and one of a kind!

What You Need

- Seventy-eight 3 x 5 index cards that are blank on both sides
- Magazines to cut up
- Glue
- A cool stamp and stamp pad
- Self-laminating sheets from the office supply store (optional)

The HOW-TO

Start by either checking a book out at the library or running a Google search on the meaning of tarot cards so that you know what every card should be called and what sorts of images should cover each and every one.

Write the names of the cards down and next to each write down the traditional imagery. Add any of your own ideas about imagery to the mix. Some cards are easy; for instance, the "Sun" card would have a picture of a sun—**duh**. But for cards like "Strength" or "Judgment," you might need to get creative. Next to the former you might write down things like **bodybuilder** or **exercise**, while the latter may inspire you to look for pictures of famous judges...like Judy. Ha!

After you've made a list of the images you're looking for, crack those magazines open and start searching. Check off the name of each card as you find ideal images for it.

Meanwhile, print out a list of the names of each of the tarot cards. Cut each name out—we're going to incorporate those into our collages.

Once you've found all your pictures, start cutting and pasting them to one side of the 3 x 5 cards; for now leave the other side blank. Take your time. Make sure you include the proper tarot name of each card into the collage so that your friend can decipher which card is which.

When you've completed all seventy-eight cards, stamp the same design on the back side of each card. You could use a mystical-looking stamp, or you could stamp your friend's initials and maybe use fancy gold ink for the job—but whatever your choice, it must appear on all seventy-eight cards, just like traditional playing cards or classic tarot cards. The outer side must not give away what is underneath!

If you want them to last an extra-long time, you can either take them to a copy shop to be laminated (see the sidebar on page 3) or you can pick up those self-laminating sheets from an office supply store and cover them that way. Even if you decide you can't afford the lamination, fear not—this is a truly one-of-a-kind gift that your pal will never, ever forget. Not even when the cards are old and tattered.

Make It an Extra-Special Gift

If your friend is a newbie tarot reader, print out a little tutorial on reading the cards, courtesy of my friend and yours, Google. Just search "how to read tarot," and you'll get a long list of sites dedicated to teaching the uninitiated. Print out a couple of pages and glue them into a  cute little notebook or staple them together zine style, then include this little book alongside your terrific tarot cards. Oh, and don't forget to tie the new deck up in a pretty bow.

• • • •

Project #2:
A Homemade Personalized Coloring Book

This is a silly, kooky, personal gift. Before you go off and say
"That's for kids," think again. Our coloring book screams "fun!"

What You Need

- Tracing paper

- Permanent black marker

- Plain white paper

- Stapler

The HOW-TO

If you're among the lucky who are naturally good drawers, throw that tracing paper away and just start sketching simple black-and-white line drawings. But if you're like me and you can't really draw all that well on your own, pick up the tracing paper. There is no shame in tracing!

The topic will depend entirely on who the gift is for. If the pal loves horses, trace or draw pictures of horses. If your friend worships emo bands, start drawing or tracing pictures of her favorites! Shoes? No sweat—make a shoe coloring book. Whatever the subject matter—fashion, soccer greats, Prince William—find pictures online or in magazines and just trace over them with clean, black lines. You can add text to the bottom to tell a story, or you could provide captions for each picture, or you could just leave them blank. Don't forget to make a cover, too, perhaps incorporating your pal's name into the title of the book.

Take your tracing paper or original drawings to a copy shop and photocopy them on to your blank paper. If you're copying tracing paper, place a piece of white paper behind the tracing paper on the bed of the copy machine so you get a bright white backdrop to your coloring pages. You could even copy these drawings on to newsprint for that old-school, little-kid-coloring-book feel. Copy the front cover of your book on to cardstock and do the same for the back cover.

Put the pages in order, add the covers, and staple. Do so by adding three staples in the left margin on your book: one at the top, one centered, and one at the bottom.

This is a great gift idea if you need to make multiple presents, because you could effortlessly make two or more copies of the coloring pages while you're at the copy shop.

Make It an Extra-Special Gift

C'mon, throw in the crayons! A small pack costs less than a buck and will really make this present zing. Throw the coloring book and the crayons into a manila envelope decorated with stickers and doodles, and you've got yourself one way cool, way wild present! Or how about adding a box of supercool colored pencils? You could even take the pencils out of their ordinary box and wrap them up sleeping bag style in a lovely little scrap of fabric, tied into a bow with a ribbon. Sweet!

Project #3: Bizarro Girly Pencils

This one is weird but so fun and, really, a pretty cheap gift for any of your school friends. We're gonna transform a measly boring ol' pencil into a hilarious gift.

What You Need

- 1-inch doll head (available at any craft store)
- Really, really small scraps of fleece or felt
- Two ½-inch pom-poms (also available at the craft store)
- A pipe cleaner
- A pencil
- Glue

The HOW-TO

If your doll head has a wire protruding from its neck, remove it (it should pull out effortlessly). Now add a dab of glue to the top and sides of the pencil eraser, then push it into the doll's neck hole. See, it's already looking weird—and now we're gonna add a scarf and some earmuffs!

Cut the piece of fleece so that it is 5 inches long and only 1/2 inch wide. Snip the ends multiple times to create fringe, about 1/2 inch long. Now tie the fabric around the "neck" of the pencil doll. Secure this with a drop of glue.

Glue a pom-pom to each ear of your doll head. Next, snip the pipe cleaner with a pair of scissors so it's the perfect length to reach from pom-pom to pom-pom, then glue it down to the top of the doll head.

Voilá! Teeny-tiny dolly earmuffs on a crazy-fun pencil doll!

Make It an Extra-Special Gift

Those doll heads usually come in small bags of six or eight. Make a ton of girly pencils, but don't make them all wintry cold! Get creative. Grab your felt scraps and your random sequins and glue, and make them adorable hats! Sweet jewelry! Ponchos! You name it. Then take a couple of girly pencils and tie them together with a ribbon, and you have a wonderfully fun, supercheap little gift for your bestest school pals. And if you want to get extra-extra special, include one or two girly pencils with the sketchbook or spiral notebook we made in Chapter 2. Now **that's** a gift!

Project #4:
A charming chalice

What's a chalice, you ask? It's a
fancy word for a cup, and it is
often also referred to as a goblet.
Now you can make your friend or
loved one a fancy, one-of-a-kind
chalice in no time at all. It makes
for a silly little gift, but honestly,
it's fairly useful. Even if the
recipient doesn't want to drink
from it, he or she can store it on
a nightstand and stash coins or
jewelry in it.

What You Need

- The most ornate and large plastic stemmed cup you can
  find (try party supply stores)

- Good multipurpose glue

- Paint pens or, if you have a steady hand, some acrylic paint and a thin brush

- Any number of sequins, beads, pipe cleaners, buttons, ribbons, nontoxic glitter, fake flowers, and the like

The How-To

This one's really basic. Start by writing your friend's name in fancy script on the cup. Then start gluing stuff to the cup. Decorate till you can barely see the cup anymore! Wind a ribbon or pipe cleaner up around the stem. Add bows. Lovely faux flowers. Glitter. Cover that thing in crafty goodness. Let it dry and wrap it up in tissue paper to protect it till you give it away.

Make It an Extra-Special Gift

You could make several of these glasses, matching but each a little different, and then instead of writing your friend's name on the glass, write what each should be a vessel for. I'm talking about words like **Rings** or **Necklaces** or **Barrettes**. Your pal can then display all her jewelry out on her dresser in these fabulous and charming chalices.

● ● ● ●

Project #5: Schmooza

What better way to say "You're my pal" or even "I love you" than a handmade stuffed animal? I made one for someone I love, and she named her Schmooza, which is just about the best name ever. This thing can really take any form—it's limited only by your imagination. And by the way, I made Schmooza completely by hand, no machine involved, and she still lives on today in great shape, years later. Just take your time and have patience.

What You Need

- Cotton fabric
- Felt bits for the face parts

- A bag of poly stuffing

- Needle and thread

- A piece of blank paper and pencil

- Pins

- Embroidery thread (optional)

- Buttons (optional)

The HOW-TO

Draw out the shape of the creature you'd like to make on a blank piece of paper. Make it the size you want your Schmooza to be, plus an inch all the way around to allow for the seam. You can get wild and make ears or a tail; get creative. But try to avoid really sharp, tight curves, as they can be hard to stuff later.

Cut your fabric into two equal pieces (larger than your creature will be, natch) and place them together, the right side of both pieces of fabric facing inward. Place the paper pattern you just made on the fabric and pin it down. Cut out the shape with a good pair of scissors.

Remove the paper pattern and set it aside. You're done with it for now, but you may want to keep it for future Schmoozas.

Now is the best time to create the face—while you can still get to the "inside" of the Schmooza. So decide which piece is going to be the face and then get crackin'. You can use felt shapes and stitch them. You can use buttons as eyes or a nose. You can embroider X's for eyes or for some other feature. It doesn't have to be elaborate. The Schmooza I made has just a simple felt mouth and two black-and-white felt eyes.

Once you're happy with the face, place your two pieces of fabric back together, with the right sides of the fabric facing inward. Pin these together all the way around. Thread and knot your needle, then get sewing. I think a tight, straight stitch, half an inch in from the edge does nicely. (See the sidebar on page 12 for instructions.) Stop before you get all the way around, making sure you leave a sizable enough opening to be able to stuff this guy up—at least 3 inches is necessary, maybe more. When it's all stitched up except for that opening, turn it right side out.

Isn't it cute!?

Now start pushing the filling in. If you need to get into nooks and crannies (or ears and tails), use the end of a spoon or a butter knife. These things always need more filling than you think, so go for it and push it to the limit.

All you have to do now is sew up the last hole, where you pushed the stuffin' through. Do this with a very teeny-tiny hemstitch. (See the sidebar on page 42 for instructions.)

Kiss it. Hug it. Then give it away.

Make It an Extra-Special Gift

I think this gift really should be delivered in a box made to be like a bed inside. Add a tissue paper blanky and pillow, and toss in a note, something that lets the givee know that you made this, with love, by hand.

• • • • •

CHAPTER FIVE

rock-'n'-roll gifts

. . . .

Most everyone has a friend or family member who loves music. I mean **loves** music. These gifts are for that person.

. . . .

Project #1: Record coasters

This is a really wild gift for a music lover because it's insanely practical and yet way cool. It's also a great way to use old scratched records you pick up at the local thrift store. Do not—I repeat, do **not**—use perfectly good records for this project; you will just anger the music lover.

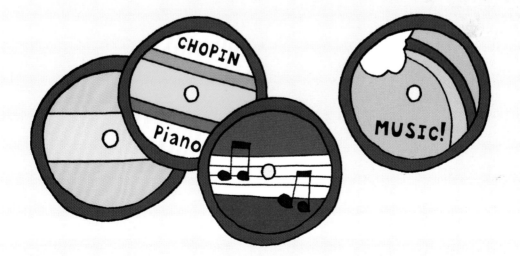

What You Need

- An oven, preheated to a low 200 degrees

- Five or six scratched-up records that have perfectly good "centers" or labels

- Spray lacquer or spray polyurethane

- Glue

- 1/4 yard of felt (alternately, you could use a package of those little felt circles that have sticky backs and are sold as "furniture protectors," available at most home improvement stores)

The How-To

Make these coasters one at a time. Take your first record out of the paper jacket and paper sleeve. Put the record directly on the oven rack of the preheated oven for two minutes and then check it. Is it soft but not yet flimsy? If so, take it out. If not, leave it in for another minute and check it again. Always watch your record and oven carefully, as you don't want it to melt and drip.

When it's ready, take the record out of the oven and start cutting the center label out, all the way around. The record will be warm to the touch, but as long as it's not melted, it won't be so hot that you will burn yourself. Warming the record makes it pliable enough to cut fairly easily, but you **must** work fast, for it will harden again quickly. Leave about an eighth of an inch of black vinyl around the label as you cut. When you've cut out your first "coaster," put it aside and start on the next one, placing it in the oven, but again watching it very carefully. Keep going until you've cut out five or six. When you have enough, turn the oven off.

Now take your coasters outside. Spread out a large piece of newspaper. Choose which side of the record label is the better side to feature and lay the labels out with the chosen side facing up. Spray them with the lacquer or polyurethane and let them dry. Spray them again and let them dry again. You may even want to spray them a third time, since this is the junk that will protect them from watery drinks. When the disks have completely dried and you're satisfied with the coating, cut out several felt circles, making them just a touch smaller than the label coasters. Apply a touch of glue to the underside of each coaster and affix a felt circle. When the glue is dried, you are **finito**.

don't throw away those record covers!

Turn to page 28 and check out the sketchbook/notebook craft project. You could make your loved one a coaster and sketchbook matching set!

Project #2:
The Greatest Guitar Strap

Got a big sister who strums the night away? A friend who is a burgeoning rock star? Or maybe your dad or uncle can't give up his dream of music stardom. This is the gift for them.

Now, it's true, you could make your own guitar strap from scratch—I've even seen a knitting pattern for one. But to make sure that it's sturdy enough to hold up even the heaviest electric guitar, I like to start with the cheapest, plainest guitar strap I can find, something so unassuming that it's downright boring. And then I attack it with crafty zest to make it the perfect accoutrement for my specific rock star pal.

What You Need

- A plain, cheap guitar strap (go to one of those supersize music shops)

- Needle and thread

- Ribbons and/or rickrack (that's the squiggly ribbon)

- Any number of small decorations, such as buttons, fake flowers, lace, sequins, beads, patches, faux pearls, feathers, pom-poms, and more

- Fabric glue

The HOW-TO

Think out your design before you start gluing or sewing—really think about the givee of such a cool gift. Do they like things flashy? If so, you just must incorporate sequins! If they're crafty themselves, consider using the buttons, perhaps making them look like flowers with ribbon petals. Maybe your friend has a flowy, earthy style. If so, think about this: Sew ribbons along the length of the strap but stitch them only about halfway down. Then the ribbons can wave in the breeze (or the wind machine!). If the recipient is very glamorous, use silk ribbon and beads and faux pearls. You can sew on ribbons and lace and patches and sequins. You can glue on faux pearls, pom-poms, and feathers. The point is to make it a one-of-a-kind and totally spot-on gift.

Project #3:
MP3 Player or Cell Phone Case

Everyone you know has a cell phone or
an MP3 player (or they want one badly),
right? This little crafty present is
basically a teeny-tiny carrying case for
these sorts of gadgets. I made one of
these for my pal Keva for her birthday,
and it got squeals of delight, which,
if you think about it, is the perfect
response to any handmade present.

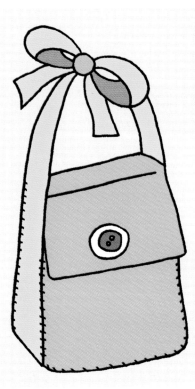

What You Need

- ⅛ yard of felt

- Approximately 1 ½ feet of ribbon, the width of which should
  be similar to the width of the gadget

- Straight pins

- A single, incredibly cute button

- A small piece of stick-on Velcro

- A drop or two of fabric glue

- Needle and embroidery thread in a contrasting color

- A monogram patch or fake flower (optional)

The HOW-TO

Different brands of cell phones and MP3 players are different dimensions, so to get the precise measurements, either go online and get the dimensions for the exact model, secretly measure your pal's gadget, or just wing it, make the case a little bigger than you think it needs to be.

The first piece of felt should be cut to the size of the gadget, plus an additional 1/2 inch all the way around. The second piece of felt needs to be cut to the same width dimensions, but the length should be 2 inches longer than the first piece (the extra 2 inches are for the flap). For example, if I were to make this for a classic iPod, my first piece of felt would be 3 1/4 by 5 1/4 inches and my second piece of felt would be 3 1/4 by 7 1/4 inches.

Because felt doesn't fray, you don't need to turn the fabric right side in to sew it, only to turn it right side out again when you're done. No sirree. You can just sew along the edges. But wait! We're not going to sew felt piece to felt piece. We're going to add a ribbon between the two pieces, giving this bag depth and room.

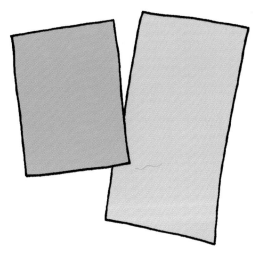

Start by taking the shorter piece of felt and pinning three sides to the ribbon's edge. Your ribbon should be centered so that equal lengths go straight up from the left and right sides. The top of the felt rectangle should be left unpinned.

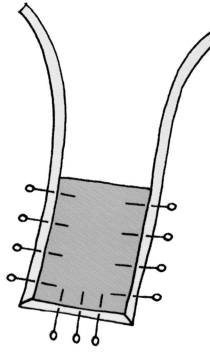

Thread and knot your needle and then start sewing the ribbon edge to the felt edge along where you pinned. Do this with small, slightly angled stitches, keeping about a quarter inch from the edge at all times. When you've sewn the ribbon to the three sides, knot your thread and cut.

Now take the other piece of felt in hand and pin the three shortest sides to the ribbon's other edge, leaving the long end open (because, remember, this is the flap). Sew the ribbon to the felt just as you did the first time. Look! You've made a little bag!

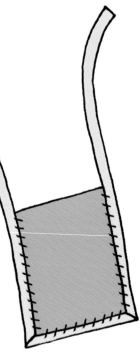

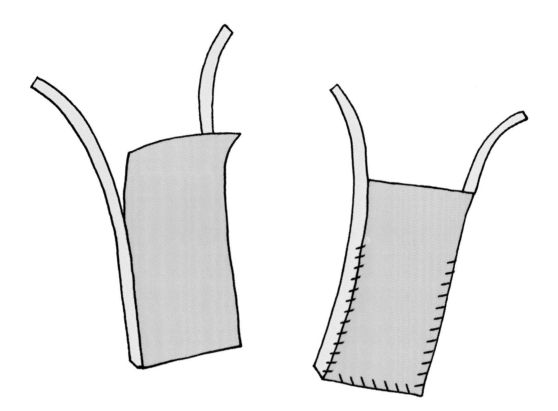

But what to do with the ribbon ends? Why, they become the handle! Simply tie them into a knot and then a bow.

Now for the flap. You can leave it squared off, or you can trim it into a triangular shape. Sew the button on to the front of the flap—it's just for show. We're actually going to secure our bag's flap with Velcro. Attach one side of the Velcro to the underside of the flap and the corresponding piece of Velcro to the front of the bag. Affix the Velcro with a drop of fabric glue. If you want to add any décor to the front of your bag, now is the time. Stitch on a fake flower, sew on a monogram patch—anything you'd like. Or simply leave it as is.

It's a gift with form and function.

●　●　●　●

CHAPTER SIX

pet-lovin' gifts

For the person whose pet means the mostest to them, give them
a gift for their animal—or create these li'l ol' gifts for your own
pet friends.

Project #1:
cute-'n'-cuddly cat Toys

This one's so easy to make—and inexpensive, too. You
can either give this to your cat as a gift or you can give
it to a cat lover friend, for their pet. Either way,
you'll make an animal happy.

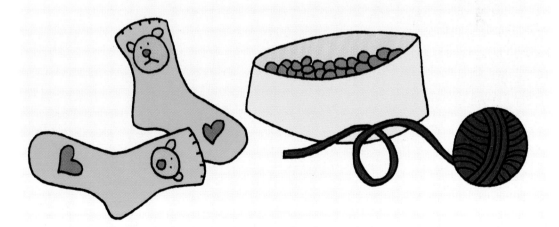

What You Need

- One or two pairs of teeny-tiny baby socks (you can buy them new or used, from a secondhand baby shop)

- Dried catnip (the pet store will have this, but even supermarkets usually carry it in the pet aisle)

- Needle and thread

- Straight pins

- A piece of cardstock or any sturdy paper

The How-To

This really works best if you have an extra set of hands, so enlist a friend to help with this project. It will take only a moment of their time. One person should hold the teeny-tiny opening of the sock as wide as possible. The other person should roll up the piece of cardstock into a funnel shape and then pour the dried catnip into the sock through the makeshift funnel. Push the catnip down with your fingers, then add some more—you want the sock packed fairly tight. Pin the opening closed and proceed to the next sock.

When you've stuffed all the socks, thread and knot your needle. Stitch the opening of each sock closed with a basic stitch, keeping your stitches close together so no nip leaks out. Remove the pins and pack your little playthings in a tiny box with a ribbon.

Purr-fect!

• • • •

Project #2:
Pet Portraits

Do you have a friend or family member who thinks of their pet as their child, or at least as a member of the family? Then perhaps this gift is for them. You could use a digital camera or borrow your parents' camera, or you could even use a disposable camera from the drugstore. It doesn't matter, they all work.

What You Need

- A camera
- A frame
- A doggy treat

The HOW-TO

Enlist a friend or sibling to help out and wrangle the pet for the photo while you concentrate on shooting the pic. Start by coming up with some excuse to pet-watch for a short while. Now, don't go anywhere the pet can get away from you. Another room is as far as you need to be with this animal. Maybe try laying out a blanket or piece of material, or simply bringing their bed into the room where you are setting up the picture.

Try to get the animal to pose, and by that I mean to just sit or lie down. Don't ever try to coerce an animal into doing something it's uncomfortable with or doesn't normally do. The point is to catch the little bugger in its natural, beautiful state!

When the pet is ready for the photo shoot, snap away. Take as many pictures as you can, then you can pick the best one later. If the animal is frightened by the flash, then by all means turn it off! Open a window and try for natural light.

When you're all done shooting, give the animal a treat.

Now get your photos developed (or, if they are digital, upload them to your computer). When they're ready, look them all over and pick the very best one of the bunch. Now take that negative (or digital file) and have the photo shop enlarge it to the size of your frame, either a 5 x 7 or an 8 x 10 or even 12 x 14. Once you get the print back, write the date on the back side and sign the back, like any good artist should. Plop it in the frame, and you have a superspecial pet-lovin' portrait, perfect for your givee!

● ● ● ●

Project #3: Pet First-Aid Kit

Every pet owner should have one of these. They're easy to put together. Grab a sturdy shoe-size box or a small handled bag and get as many of the things on the following list as you can. By the way, I got the list from the Humane Society.

What You Need

* Something to house the kit, such as the aforementioned shoe box or a small bag with a handle

* Rectal thermometer (I know, I know)

* Small tub or tube of petroleum jelly

- Instant hot and cold compresses

- Adhesive tape (to secure bandages)

- Round-tipped scissors

- Splints

- Tweezers

- Alcohol swabs

- A mild antibacterial soap (for cleaning wounds)

- Sterile gauze pads

- Cotton swabs

- Rubber bulb syringe (it's sort of like a plastic dropper that new moms use for sucking snot from a baby's nose—really!—and can come in handy for a pet owner who needs to remove things from a doggy's or kitty's nose)

The HOW-TO

Collect as many of the first-aid items listed as possible and arrange them in the kit box or bag. You could also go to the Humane Society's website and print out the instructions for treating specific injuries, then include that in this kit as well. Another great thing to add would be a card listing the phone number for Poison Control for pets, contact information for the local animal hospital, and the vet's number and address. You can laminate this card (yea for the ever-useful laminating machine!) at the local copy shop; that way, it's waterproof and extra sturdy. It may be a little dark for a present, but this shows thoughtfulness and a genuine love and desire for animals' well-being.

• • • •

CHAPTER SEVEN

krazy kits

• •

Instead of offering up a single gift or two for that special someone, you can compile a list of like-minded, smaller gifts into something wild, unusual, useful, and wholly personal. I call this—drumroll, please—"The Kit." (Okay, it's not the most creative name. You can probably think of something better, huh?)

On the following pages, you'll find a collection of easy-to-assemble kits, but I've also included combinations of various projects in this book that will make up tremendously cool gifty kits extraordinaire. From there, you can create your own kits—like a polka kit for that friend who's been aching to try polka dancing.

Project #1: car wash Kit

This is the perfect gift for that person who needs a great big ol' hint that their car is a filthy mess. Someone like your dad or a big sister or your uncle Verne. If your recipient has a car, they need to clean it eventually, so this gift is practical, too. All of the goods below can be bought at an auto supply store, and most can be found at a general mega-mart. Oh, and you don't have to get all of the suggested items—figure out a budget for your gift and just buy what you can.

What You Need

- An attractive but sturdy galvanized metal bucket (or a plastic bucket from the dollar store)

- Car sponges and/or chammy cloths

- Car-washing soap

- Car wax

- Glass cleaner

- A squeegee

- Car air freshener

The HOW-TO

It doesn't get any easier than this. Pile all the stuff you got into the bucket and tie a bow on it. Tie a tag to the handle that explains that this stuff is for washing the car and wish the givee a happy day.

Make It an Extra-Special Gift

You could make your own cute and funny labels for the bottles of soap, wax, and glass cleaner. Print them out on the computer and glue them over the originals with a glue stick. Something like UNCLE CHARLIE'S HANDY-DANDY SPECIAL CAR SOAP would do nicely. You could also write up some coupons for free car washes and include them inside the bucket. This is a great gift to go in on with someone else too. Share the expense and then share the free car-washing duty!

Project #2: The Love Letter Kit

E-mail has taken over our lives—it's a sad truth! Gone are the days of letters on pretty paper, for the most part. But isn't it fun to get a letter in the mail once in a while? Inspire someone to write with a cool-cool gift of stationery.

I suggest going one step further and giving a gift that encourages the best kind of letter writing: the love letter. My ideas should just be a springboard for your imagination. When I say you need a box, look around your room or at the dollar store for a cool but cheap box of any kind. If I forgot something that you think would be ideal for a love letter kit, throw it in. Imagine yourself back in time, like in Jane Austen's day (she wrote **Pride and Prejudice** and **Emma** and all those other smart, lovey books) and craft a wondrous, romantic box de love.

What You Need

- A box (my favorite for this project is one of those clear plastic boxes that holds cookies or brownies at the grocery store; many grocery stores also use them to house a four-pack of fruit)

- Some cute stationery (yes, you can make your own with some nice paper and a stamp or with old maps or even with a handmade collage border that you can then photocopy at the copy shop)

- Glue stick

Optional Items

You don't have to include all of these possibilities and feel free to think up some cool things of your own.

- Those free tiny vials of sample perfume (to scent the letters, silly) or a very, very small bottle of spray perfume

- A rosy red lipstick (for kissing the letters, lovah!)

- A fancy pen or pencil, preferably with large feather on top

- Stamp pad and stamp of recipient's initial and/or of a heart

- Wax seal with initial and accompanying wax (you can find this old-school accoutrement at an art or craft store)

- Adorable little stickers in red and pink

- Small chocolates

- Rose petals, fake or real

- Confetti (just because confetti is so darn fun)

The How-To

Either on the computer or with a marker and a piece of paper, create a label for the box. It should be simple, something along the lines of THE LOVE LETTER KIT, or you can get silly and use THE SMOOCHIEST LOVEY-DOVEY LETTER KIT AKA A ROMANTIC BOX O' LOVE. You could even include the recipient's name in the title. Cut it out and affix it to the top of your box with the glue stick.

Arrange all your goodies inside the box and tie it up with a ribbon. If you happen to have a fake flower hanging around, tie that into the bow. De-luxe, I say.

Make It an Extra-Special Gift

Hit the used bookstore in your area and ask for a book of love poetry. Don't be embarrassed, it's way sweet. You could create a book cover for the tome, or you could leave it as is, especially if it has a pretty cover. Include this book with your Love Letter Kit, and you've served your friend well.

• • • •

Project #3:
A Modern Embroidery Kit

Embroidery is **très** hip
these days. Instead
of embroidering Old
English odes to home
and hearth, people
are stitching up
tattoo-inspired art,
retro nursery designs,
mod patterns, even
portraits. And, whoa,
have you checked out
how cheap embroidery
floss is? We're talking pocket
change. So, the perfect gift for the
newbie embroiderer? A kit! But this
is also a fantastic prezzie for even
an experienced stitcher.

What You Need

- A supercool three-ring binder notebook

- Three or more clear plastic binder envelopes—the kind that
  would normally hold your pencils and erasers

- A piece of felt

- A hole punch

- A muncha-buncha embroidery floss in wowsa colors

- Embroidery needles of varying size

- A small pair of thread scissors

- Some embroidery transfer paper (from a sewing shop) and/or a small, cool embroidery transfer

- A small embroidery hoop

- A long piece of ribbon

- A small, plain hanky

The HOW-To

Put all the thread and the little pair of scissors in the plastic pockets of the binder envelopes. Put the transfer paper in another one. Add the hanky to yet another. Click the pockets into your binder. Cut a piece of felt slightly smaller than the notebook. With your hole punch, poke holes in the felt so it fits in the binder like a piece of paper would. Weave the tips of the needles into the felt—this is where they will be stored. Felt is a great holder for needles in the absence of a pincushion.

Attach the hoop to the binder with the ribbon: Just poke the ribbon end through the binder rings, centering it so that an equal length of ribbon pokes out from the top and the bottom. Loop the ribbon through the embroidery hoop, then tie it in a bow.

Your gift is complete! The recipient has all the junk they need to make their first project: a sweet handkerchief.

Make It an Extra-Special Gift

If you know how to embroider already and your giftee doesn't, include a coupon for a free lesson (with you)! If neither of you knows how to embroider, hit the library for a book on basic stitches. Photocopy the pages and punch holes in them so they, too, fit inside your binder.

Thoughtful **and** practical!

• • • •

Project #4: Unique Scrapbook-Stamp Kit

Perhaps you have a friend who is pretty crafty and gets into her scrapbooking sessions like most teens get into their Xbox. Or perhaps your mom or an aunt has the passion for the scrap. This is the gift for them. You're gonna create one-of-a-kind, superspecial stamps that they can use till their big scrapbooking hearts are content. As for the buttons, check thrift stores, antique malls, swap meets, and, yes, sewing stores. Vintage ones work best, but there are cool new buttons out there in the world—you just have to have your eyes wide open.

What You Need

* Single, odd, patterned buttons that have texture

* A bag of different-size craft corks (you can find this at a craft store)

- Glue

- Inked stamp pads in beautiful colors

The How-To

Match up buttons to corks—each cork end should be slightly smaller than its corresponding button. Then glue the button's back side to the cork end with your glue. Make as many stamps as you have buttons. Give them time to dry.

Put the dry stamps and the pads into a box and add a note that advises the user to stack some paper towels under the paper before they begin stamping because that will give the hard button stamp a little extra give, so it'll make a prettier impression. And remind your pal or loved one to wipe the "stamps," aka the buttons, clean with a wet sponge before putting them away or changing colors. Hey, you could even throw a sponge into the gift box and attach the note to the sponge with a safety pin.

Make It an Extra-Special Gift

Test-drive the stamps on a strip of pretty paper before giving the gift, then include the strip of paper in the gift box. That way, the user can see how beautiful and extraordinary this totally unique gift really is. Just roll up the strip of paper like a scroll and tie it up with a small piece of ribbon.

• • • •

Project #5: The Hula Kit

For the girl who has everything...or just likes to dance. This kit gives your pal or loved one all she needs to learn to do the hula! You could adapt this same concept to most any kind of dance: For a disco kit, for example, just replace the Hawaiian music and clothes with '70s music and attire. For a tango kit, go for a Latin mix of accessories. Use your imagination and get your friends to kick up their heels (or sway their hips!).

By the way, you don't need **everything** on the following list. Nab whatever you can round up. But at the very least try to get some of the outfit items and the dance instructions. Oh, and most of this stuff is available at your neighborhood party supply store or costume shop.

What You Need

- Plastic flower lei

- Hula skirt

- Plastic tropical flowers (for her hair!)

- A CD of Hawaiian music (or download a handful of Don Ho songs and burn them to a disc)

- Cute bikini

- A hula video and/or a hula book (see "The How-To" section for cheap alternatives)

- Shell necklace

- Cheap sunglasses

- Plastic coconut or tiki cup

- Inflatable palm tree

- Cheap beach bag

- Map of Hawaii

The HOW-TO

Many of the grass skirts you can buy also come with tiny little booklets on hula dancing—you might not even need to put one together. But if you're going to forgo the skirt or if the skirt doesn't come with an instructional booklet, don't fret. Hit your local library and look up "hula." Once you find a good book, do one of two things. Either photocopy the best pages or write out the instructions by hand and draw a few accompanying pictures. Make a cute Hawaiian cover for your handwritten or copied pages with fun tropical wrapping paper, an old, scratched Hawaiian record cover, or a bamboolike place mat, then either staple or spiral bind (at the copy shop) it all together. Voilá, you've got a cheap-cheap "How to Hula" book!

Individually wrap all your stuff in the map of Hawaii—it's the perfect wrapping paper for this project! Pile all the wrapped gifts you've collected into the beach bag. You could even tie a piece of sea grass ribbon to the handle. I bet no one else will be giving your friend a hula kit. Your gift will be so totally unique!

Project #6: The Haute Hot Choco Kit

Everyone loves chocolate, right? So this is the perfect wintry gift to give the person who has everything. This kit includes the makings for at least three different types of hot chocolate, and we'll make recipe cards to instruct the givee on how to proceed into delicious, delirious chocolate overload!

What You Need

- A large bar of quality bittersweet chocolate and/or Mexican bricks of chocolate

- A bar of white chocolate

- A small carrot peeler (for shaving the chocolate)

- 1 tablespoon allspice

- 1 tablespoon cinnamon

- 1 tablespoon ancho chili powder

- 1 tablespoon chipotle chili powder

- Marshmallows

- A couple of candy canes (if it's the season)

- A small bottle of vanilla extract

- A mug or two

- Plain index cards

- One very small cellophane bag and one medium cellophane bag (you can usually find these at baking supply stores or candy-making supply stores or at the local dollar shop; if you can't find them, plastic sandwich bags can be used instead)

- A basket or box to hold the goods

The HOW-TO

Mix up the allspice, cinnamon, and the chili powders and pour them into the small cellophane bag. Then seal it with a twisty tie or ribbon. Toss the marshmallows into the larger cellophane bag and add a twisty tie or ribbon. Arrange the chocolate bars, peeler, spice bag, marshmallow bag, candy canes, vanilla extract, and mugs in the basket or box.

Write out the following recipes on each of the index cards. You can laminate them at the local copy shop or with self-adhesive laminating sheets from an office supply store. Or you can leave them as is.

Now for the recipes...

Classic Cocoa

Pour 1 cup of milk into a heavy-bottomed pan and warm over medium heat. Shave 2 ounces of chocolate with the peeler. After the milk has warmed for 2–4 minutes, toss in the shaved chocolate and stir. Keep stirring. Just before the milk boils, remove the pan from the heat, transfer to a mug, and garnish with whipped cream and/or marshmallows. Makes 1 cup of yummy cocoa!

Minty Cocoa

Follow the recipe for Classic Cocoa, but garnish with a candy cane stirrer. The minty oils will melt into your cocoa, giving it zest and zing!

Vanilla & Choco Cocoa

Follow the recipe for Classic Cocoa, but this time add 1 teaspoon of vanilla extract to the milk when you add the chocolate. Extra richness and depth!

Spicy Hot Chocolate

Follow the recipe for Classic Cocoa, but add a large pinch of the spice mix to the milk with the chocolate. (Beware, there is hot-hot-hot chili powder in that there spice mix!)

Hot White Chocolate

Mix 1/2 cup of milk and 1/2 cup of heavy cream in a heavy-bottomed pan and warm over medium heat. Shave 2 ounces of white chocolate with your peeler and toss it in with the liquid after it's been warming for 2–4 minutes. Stir. Keep stirring until it's just about to boil and then, quicklike, remove it. Garnish with marshmallows!

Done? Toss those cards in the box and wrap it up.

We Love Gift Kits!

Kits are great gifts, as we already established. You can make a lot of very special gift kits by combining a few inexpensively purchased things with a few homemade things. Check it out:

Book Lover's Kit

Combine a great used book with a homemade book cover (make it out of anything and wrap the book like you do your schoolbooks), then add a bookmark from page 25.

Rock Star Kit

Combine a great CD, a makeshift "Beginner's Guide to Guitar," a handful of cheap guitar picks, and the guitar strap from page 76.

Music Lover's Kit

Combine a homemade mix CD, the CD case from page 28 and the MP3 player cover from page 78.

The Back-to-School Kit
Combine homemade notebooks and the day planner from page 28 with the girly pencil toppers from page 64.

The Doggy Lover's Kit
Combine a great big bone from the pet store, the Pet First-Aid Kit from page 87, and a pet portrait from page 85.

The Cat Lover's Kit
Combine the catnip sock toys from page 83, a fluffy collar from the pet store, and a pet portrait from page 85.

The Cozy Nights Kit
Combine some yummy herbal tea bags, the hand warmer from page 39, the rice neck roll from page 43, and the slipper socks from page 47.

The Tea Lover's Kit
Combine some nice herbal tea bags, some mismatched but pretty teacups from the thrift store, and the teacup candles from page 50.

CHAPTER EIGHT

cool cards

Sometimes a handmade card elevates an ordinary gift to extraordinary. And at other times a handmade card is all you need to give. So don't forget the card....

Project #1:
Button Garden card

What You Need

- A blank card or a piece of cardstock folded into a card shape

- An additional piece of cardstock, slightly smaller than the face of the card

- Embroidery floss in several colors

- Needle

- A couple of cool buttons

- A pencil

- Craft glue

The How-To

On the extra (smaller) piece of cardstock, lightly sketch out a drawing of flowers that incorporates the buttons as the flower buds. Place the buttons over the buds and poke the needle through the buttonholes, leaving teeny-tiny holes behind on the cardstock. Set the buttons aside for a moment.

Take the needle and poke more holes, along the lines of your drawing, spacing them out about every quarter inch—this creates a path for the thread.

When you've completed the poking, thread and knot your needle. Start from the underside of the cardstock and embroider the stems, leaves, and such by following the needle-prick holes. Make sure to finish sewing on the underside as well. Trim the thread close to the knot and then switch colors, threading and knotting your needle again. Continue until your picture is complete. Finish up by sewing the buttons in place. You should have a sweet little picture embroidered with beautiful button blooms.

Turn the embroidered cardstock over and smear a light layer of craft glue all over. Center it on the face of the card and press firmly. Let it dry and write your special message inside.

Project #2: Felt card

You know how the crafts in this book are always calling for felt? Well, you must have a load of scraps by now. Turn them into extra-fancy cards in a snap.

What You Need

- A plain, blank premade card or a sheet of cardstock cut and folded to resemble a card

- Various felt scraps

- Craft glue

The HOW-TO

Break out your creativity and preschool art skills. Think about the theme of this gift or the holiday behind it and come up with a simple icon that represents it, like a birthday cake or a heart. Or you can stick to generic good-for-all-occasions images like flowers, glowing suns, or trees. You could even choose a mod, abstract design. But the point is to cut out various shapes from the different-colored felt scraps and position them on the card. When you've made a design you like, get out the glue and start affixing the pieces to the card. You can also add ribbon trim if you like. The end result is a 3-D card with style **and** handmade panache.

• • • •

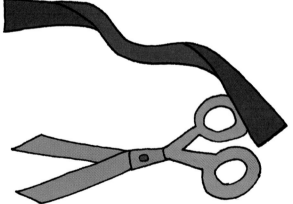

Project #3:
Puzzling Puzzle card

This is a card that's also a gift and a challenge. Essentially, you're gonna make a card and then cut it into lots of pieces—the givee has to put it together to decipher the message.

What You Need

- A sheet of cardstock

- Glue stick

- Images you like, from magazines, newspapers, or photocopied photos

The HOW-TO

Either blow up a photo on a copy machine or make a collage of pictures that covers one whole side of the cardstock. Glue it down to the cardstock. On the flip side write out your message. Feel free to add doodles or write your note in concentric circles or some other graphic pattern.

Now take your scissors and either cut the sheet into classic puzzle shapes or simple, evenly spaced squares. Take all the pieces and toss them into an envelope. Don't provide any instructions—let the givee figure it out on their own. That's half the fun!

Project #4:
Pretty Picture Card

Sometimes the best way to say what you want to say is with pictures. This is perfect for a best friend's birthday, Mother's Day, or Father's Day—you know, **special** events.

What You Need

- A sheet of 10 x 14 inch cardstock (you can usually get just a single sheet of this sort of paper at the copy shop)

- Four small photos or color copies of photos

- 2 feet of 1/4 - to 1/2-inch-wide ribbon

- Ruler

- Craft glue

The HOW-TO

Cut the sheet of cardstock in half, into 5 x 14 inch pieces. Fold one piece in half lengthwise once, then again. Now you should have four equal quadrants. Unfold and then refold the cardstock into an accordion-style fold utilizing the creases you just made. Deepen the creases by rubbing the edge of the ruler along each newly folded crease.

Open up the sheet once again. You now see four distinct and equal quadrants. Center a single picture in each of these quadrants. Affix them with glue.

Now measure each side of each picture and cut a length of ribbon for every measurement. You'll use the ribbons to "frame" each picture. Glue the ribbon down along the edges of each picture. You could add a date or a quote in pen just below each picture, or you could leave it blank underneath—whatever you think suits the occasion. Sign the last quadrant and refold. Now **that's** a card worth saving.

* * * *

Project #5:
Paper Airplane Card

Sure, this doesn't fit into an envelope—but then, it doesn't need a postman to get where it needs to go!

What You Need

- 8 ½ x 11 inch sheet of paper

- Pen

- Ruler

The HOW-TO

1. Position your paper in front of you with the shorter side on top. Fold the upper left and upper right corners of the paper in toward the center so they form a point at the top.

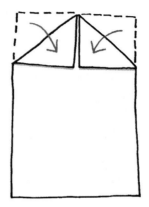

2. Measure down 1 inch from where the corners meet in the center of the page and mark that spot with a pen dot. Now fold the top point down till it matches up with the dot.

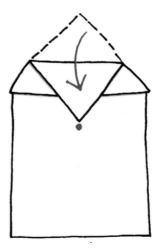

3. Once again, fold the upper left and upper right corners in toward the center so they form a point, just like you did in step 1.

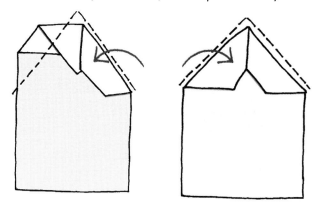

4. Fold just the tip of the point up.

5. Fold the paper in half vertically.

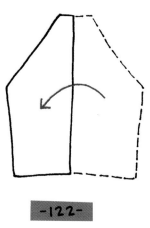

6. Fold out each wing.

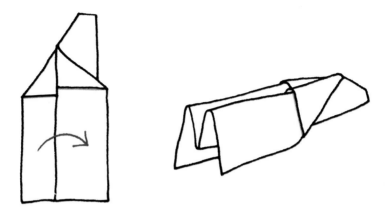

7. Voilá! You have yourself an airplane!

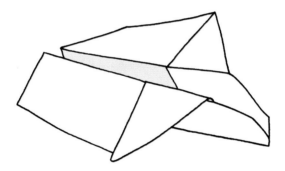

Write your message on the wings. If you need a flat surface to write on, make a small X in pencil on the wings and then unfold. Write your message out where the X's are, then refold the plane. Then fly it over to the lucky givee!

● ● ● ●

Project #6:
Way cool Make-It-Your-own Envelopes

Already have a cool card, just need a jazzy envelope? Here you go.

What You Need

- A boring ol' white envelope in the size you need

- A cool piece of paper, may it be wrapping paper, a map, old wallpaper, a doily, newspaper, whatever—as long as it's paper

- Pencil

- Glue stick

The HOW-TO

Carefully take apart the seams of the boring white envelope, opening it up till it's a completely flat piece of paper. Lay it down on the reverse side of your paper of choice and trace around the edges of the envelope. Cut out the unfolded envelope shape from the cool paper.

Now copy the folds of the original white envelope until your cool paper looks like a real, genuine envelope. Seal the seams with a glue stick, except for the last flap. After you enclose your card, seal the flap with either a glue stick or a small sticker.

• • • •

small gifts with big impact

Sometimes a gift is just a slip of paper. When that's the case, make sure to cloak it in the coolest envelope, such as the Way Cool Make-Your-Own Envelope (at left). The following is a short list of great "slip gifts."

DOG WASHING COUPON

*Homemade coupons for dog washing, housecleaning, foot rubs, home-cooked dinners, or babysitting

*Tickets to a movie you and your pal are both aching to see

*Tickets in general are good: concert tickets, ballet tickets, opera tickets, rodeo tickets, museum exhibit tickets

CHAPTER NINE

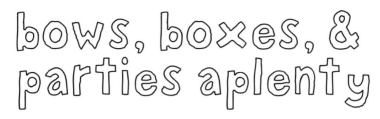

bows, boxes, & parties aplenty

. . . .

If you don't want to put your cool-cool handmade gift into a stale old shoe box or basic, boring wrap, try these alternatives that will further highlight your creative gift-giving flair.

. . . .

Alternatives to Wrapping Paper

Sometimes, no matter where you look, all you can find is Disney paper or stuffy old-lady wrapping. Where's the cool stuff when you need it? That's when it is time to rethink what wrapping paper is. And you know what? **It's just paper!** So why not use some other kind of paper to wrap up your homemade gifts? Plus, as an extra added bonus, you'll be recycling!

Other things to wrap presents with:

- Old maps

- Newspaper—bonus points for cool foreign newspapers

- Color photocopies of family photos

- Vintage wallpaper

- Finger paintings from preschool

- Magazine articles

- Bubble wrap (it cushions AND is so cool to look at!)

- A scrap of fabric or an old piece of clothing that you de-seam

- Cute dishcloths

- Paper grocery bags (you could even stamp them with a cool design)

- Last year's calendar

- Blue paper from the dry cleaner's

- Color photocopies of anything graphic like vintage game boards or gum wrappers

- Sheet music

- Tacky tabloids

- Japanese manga

- 1980s posters you pick up at the local thrift store

- Accounting ledgers

- Graph paper

- Museum guides

- Take-out menus

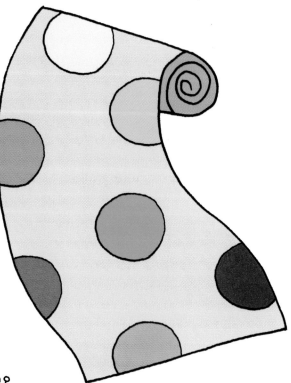

Alternatives to Boxes

You could forgo the wrapping paper altogether and just enclose your gift in a supercool box. But where to get such a thing? Look around, they're everywhere.

- Toilet paper and paper towel cardboard rolls

- Bamboo steamers (you know, those containers you get dumplings in when you go out for Chinese?)

- Take-out containers from a restaurant supply store

- Cheap lunch boxes

- Cereal boxes

- Plain, unpainted, unused paint cans from the hardware store

- The tiny metal boxes mints and candies come in

- Cigar boxes

- Clean and dry soup cans

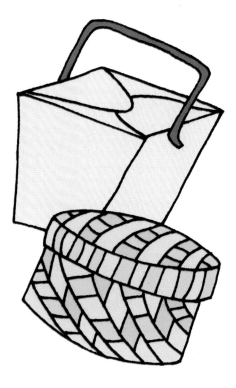

Gift-Giving Parties

When the holidays roll around and all of a sudden you've got to give two thousand gifts, it's time to rethink the whole gift-gifting process. A lot of people don't buy (or make) gifts for everyone on their lists. Instead, they have created crafty little games and parties that make gift giving a lot less costly and whole lotta fun. If your family or group of friends is just humongous, maybe you should try one of these ideas.

The Yankee Swap

My girlfriends and I have been doing a variation of this for years. Early on there were about five of us. Now the party can include as many as thirty friends.

Each guest is instructed to bring a wrapped present of a predetermined value (ours is $25 or less). As the guests enter, they pile their gifts in one area. Once everyone has arrived, each guest draws a number to see who shall "pick" first. Whoever chooses number one walks over to the pile o' presents and chooses a pretty gift. They open it and show everyone what they got. There is a lot of oohing and ahhing. But now the person who pulled number two can steal that first opened gift **or** they can open any of the beautifully wrapped presents. Anyone who is asked to give up their gift has to do so. And so on. Once you have a gift in your possession three times, the present is yours. (Or at least, that's our rule!) You never know what will be "fought" over, you never know what you'll come away with. But I promise, it's a blast.

The White Elephant Party

This is a variation on the Yankee swap. It works exactly the same way, actually, but the presents people bring can be anything they don't want anymore or really tacky, silly presents. The trick is to wrap your hideous present in really appealing wrapping so that the others will want it badly. Sneaky, eh?

Themed Gift Exchanges

This type of event is run the same way as a Yankee swap or white elephant party, but all the gifts follow the same theme. For example, at a "black-and-white party" every gift has to be white and/or black; at a book party everyone has to bring a favorite book as his or her gift.

Secret Santa

My friend Michelle's family does this come Christmastime. They call it "secret Santa," but it will work for any gift-giving holiday, so adjust the name to whatever will suit the occasion. In Michelle's house, around Thanksgiving, all family members throw their names into a bowl. Each person then draws a name from the bowl to see whom they should give to, but no one reveals whose name they picked. The recipient doesn't know whom her gift is coming from until she opens the present and the giver reveals himself. It's a fun little game and keeps costs to a minimum (because you're not buying gifts for everyone in your family).

Lucky Bags

I read about this in a magazine. It's a variation of the secret Santa idea, but instead of making or buying one big gift for your chosen person, you create a bag filled with two-dollar and three-dollar presents, all totaling no more than $15. That would be hard if you weren't such a crafty person. Think of the things you could make for two or three dollars!